AN AUSTRALIAN
CHRISTMAS COLLECTION

For Bob and the Renfrees
on both sides of the Tasman,
not forgetting H.E.R.

AN AUSTRALIAN
CHRISTMAS COLLECTION

Compiled by Gwenda Hardie

HODDER & STOUGHTON
Sydney Auckland London Toronto

Design and additional illustration by Sophie Tourrier
Design assistant, Elly Mellick

First published in 1991 by
Hodder & Stoughton (Australia) Pty Ltd
ACN 000 884 855
10-16 South Street, Rydalmere, NSW 2116

National Library of Australia
Cataloguing-in-publication entry

Hardie, Gwenda
An Australian Christmas collection
ISBN 0 340 54959 9

1. Christmas – Australia – Literary Collections.
2. Christmas music. 3. Australian literature.
I. Hardie, Gwenda
A820.8033

Typeset by Character & Caps, Sydney
Printed by The Griffin Press, Adelaide

Contents

Christmas
=IN=
Sydney

We now made a few weeks' sojourn in Sydney, which, could we have laid the dust, moderated the heat, and dismissed the mosquitoes and their assistants, would have been very pleasant; but as it was, my colonial enjoyments were limited to our usual drives, and when able to walk at all, an idle, languid stroll in the beautiful Government gardens. For some days before Christmas, in our drives near the town, we used to meet numbers of persons carrying bundles of a beautiful native shrub, to decorate the houses, in the same manner that we use holly and evergreens at home. Men, women, and children, white, brown, and black, were in the trade; and sometimes a horse approached, so covered with the bowery load he bore, that only his legs were visible, and led by a man nearly as much hidden; carts heaped up with the green and blossomed boughs came noddingly along, with children running beside them, decked out with sprays and garlands, laughing and shouting in proper Christmas jollity. I liked to see this attempt at the perpetuation of some of our ancient homely poetry of life, in this new and generally too prosaic Colony, where the cabalistic letters *£.s.d.* and RUM appear too frequently the alphabet of existence. It seemed like a good healthy memory of *home*; and I doubt not the decked-out windows and bouquet-filled chimney in many a tradesman's house gave a more home-like flavour to his beef or turkey, and aided in the remembrance of old days and old friends alike numbered with the past.

The shrub chosen as the Sydney 'Christmas' is well worthy of the honour (the rough usage it

6

receives rendering the quality of the post it occupies rather problematical, by the way). It is a handsome verdant shrub, growing from two to twelve or fifteen feet high, with leaves in shape like those of the horse-chestnut, but only two or three inches broad, with a dark green, polished, upper surface, the under one being pale. The flowers, which are irregularly star-shaped, come out in light terminal sprays, their chief peculiarity being, that they completely open whilst quite small, and of a greenish white colour; they then continue increasing in size, and gradually ripening in tint, becoming first a pearl white, then palest blush, then pink, rose-colour, and crimson: the constant change taking place in them, and the presence of all these hues at one time on a spray of half a dozen flowers, has a singularly pretty appearance. Their scent when freshly gathered is like that of new-mown hay.

Great quantities of the shrub grow in the neighbourhood of Sydney, or I should fear that such wholesale demolition as I witnessed would soon render them rare.

Mrs Charles Meredith,
1844.

DOUGLAS LOCKWOOD

WOMEN of the OUTBACK

The Murranji track is one of Australia's loneliest roads. It winds out west over black soil plains and across drummy ground from Newcastle Waters into the sunset country of the Victoria River district.

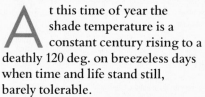

At this time of year the shade temperature is a constant century rising to a deathly 120 deg. on breezeless days when time and life stand still, barely tolerable.

And it is on such a day that a lone motorist racing to beat the monsoons into the Kimberleys is most likely to stop at the Top Springs store for fuel and refreshments.

He has come 150 miles from bitumen at Newcastle Waters without seeing a trace of habitation and he will drive 320 miles to Halls Creek before he sees another shop.

He is served with petrol and whatever else he needs by Mrs. Thelma Hawkes, whose husband Sid is on a week's buying trip to Darwin or is hauling timber from the fringes of Arnhem Land for the oasis he is building there 40 miles from his nearest neighbour.

Thelma Hawkes's watchful dog, a Queensland heeler named Lady, gets to her feet and snarls as the stranger extends his hand towards her mistress – to take his chance.

"Quiet, Lady," she says and the dog relaxes.

The motorist drives on. Mrs. Hawkes is pleased that her husband will return that night. In spite of the protection of the faithful dog and any natives who might be around, she must feel her loneliness and her helplessness if trouble came – as it did at Sundown station a fortnight ago.

She is one of the pioneer women of the West who have a burden today which is only a little lighter than when George Essex Evans wrote about them.

So this Christmas I would like you to remember them briefly.

I would like you to know that

in a land which is criss-crossed by airlines and wireless there are still women who must live for weeks, and sometimes months, of every year with a private fear in their hearts – that natural feminine instinct which rebels against isolation.

Consider for a moment while you carve the turkey whether you would like to be a woman spending this Christmas at Kulgera cattle station where Sally Bowman, her daughter Wendy and Thomas Whelan were last seen alive on December 5.

Mrs. Roy Couthard is there, a pioneer of the blood royal.

Perhaps you would like to be with Mrs. Rex Lowe, of Mt. Cavanagh, of which abandoned Sundown is an outstation, or with Mrs. Sid Staines at nearby Erldunda.

Remember that at the time of the murder an eccentric swagman called at Erldunda homestead and Mrs. Staines gave him a meal?

For most of the year these women have male company at the homestead. But there are periods varying from weeks to months during the annual muster when the men are away from home and the loyal native stockmen are out with them on the frontiers of the nation.

Even so, these places are on the beaten track. Comparatively, they are almost urban.

For extreme isolation come north with me to Roper Valley on the southern border of Arnhem Land where attractive Mrs. Julie Holt once spent an entire wet season alone while her husband Tom was cut off by floods.

Let us go farther still to the coastal mission stations of Arnhem Land where missionaries' wives like Mrs. Alf Ellison at Goulburn Island sit and wait at this time each year for cyclones which might strike their homes down. Or we can go out west to immense cattle stations like Victoria River Downs where Mrs. Daisy Quirk battles with the problems of a homestead which is really a small township. No loneliness here – the place even has a post office.

But there is no telephone and no way of communicating with neighbours except on the pedal radio "cockatoo" session.

Neighbours? Mrs. Kath Morey is 70 miles away to the north at Coolibah station, run by her husband Ted, who musters in hard riding country which requires his absence for weeks at a time.

Out east on the fringes of Simpson Desert I could take you to a homestead run by former screen star Daphne Campbell of the Overlanders. She now has four young children but she is still as lithe and brave as you knew her, battling not only isolation but the poisonous Gidyea bush which has killed hundreds of their cattle.

Her husband, Sam Calder, is manager of the station that has a name as beautiful as his wife – Argadargada. Say it slowly because nothing much else out there is beautiful unless it is the beauty of stark realism.

I would like to go again to talk with Mrs. Cant at Anthony's Lagoon in the heart of Barkly Tableland, 180 miles east of the road at Elliott.

And we could swing over from there to the Darcy family at Malpunyah Springs who never leave the Northern Territory.

But I will probably go instead to the Daly River for another yarn with blonde, petite Mrs. Nancy Polishuk.

You see, it was just after last Christmas that she came to my home in Darwin. The worst floods in the history of the Daly had washed away everything she owned.

She and her husband John were lucky to save their lives. While they watched the pouring rain and rising river one night, Nancy flashed her torch on the water, then lapping the floorboards.

It shone in the blood-red eyes of three man-eating crocodiles which were disturbed occasionally by sharks.

"Next morning we had to evacuate," Nancy said. "We loaded all our belongings into a boat and set off upstream."

"After an hour or so we had to refuel which meant stopping the motor. When we did that we were caught by the current and swept along until we hit a tree. The launch capsized and we were all thrown into the river – my daughter Marlene, aged four, my baby son Peter (14 months) and my husband John, who was washed against a tree.

"I was submerged somewhere near the children.

"I grabbed Peter instinctively and managed to reach Marlene under the water and clasp her arms around my waist.

"With the two of them hanging on, I began to frog kick to surface. We were swept downstream by the boiling current with the capsized launch following.

"I was frantic with fear and I am not a very good swimmer, but somehow I swam to that upside down boat and hung on with the kids."

Polishuk: "We drifted for six miles in an hour and were then rescued by natives."

For six days and nights the family camped in the open, lashed by terrible tropical storms. They were barefoot and they ate wallaby shot by the men. Twelve days later they went back to their mud-encrusted home and began to clean it up.

Now it is raining again and the Polishuks are watching the river. The missionaries' wives are watching the wind.

The station women are watching the roads and the faces of visitors.

Happy Christmas from the frontier land.

Drink a toast to the women of the outback.

Bush Christmas

Stuffed with pudding to his gizzard
   Uncle James lets out a snore,
Auntie Flo sprawls like a lizard
   On the back verandah floor.

Grandpa Aub sits with a flagon
   On the woodheap 'neath the gums,
And he thinks he's seen a dragon
   Where the pigs are munching plums.

Cousin Val and Cousin Harry,
   Cousin May and Cousin Fred,
Play the goat with Dulce and Larry
   By the creek below the shed.

In the scrub the cows are drowsing,
   Dogs are dreaming in the shade.
Fat and white, the mare is browsing,
   Cropping softly, blade by blade.

It is hot. Mosquitoes whirring.
   Uncle James rubs his knee:
"Flo," he whispers, "are you stirring?
   It's near time to get the tea."

David Martin

'In the Old Fashiond Way'

In June 1769 the **Endeavour**, under the command of Captain James Cook, with Banks as botanist, sailed westward from Tahiti in search of Terra Australis Incognita.
Christmas was celebrated on the way.
December 1769
24. Land in sight, an Island or rather several small ones most probably 3 Kings, so that it was conjecturd that we had Passed the Cape which had so long troubled us. Calm most of the Day: myself in a boat shooting in which I had good success, killing cheifly several Gannets or Solan Geese so like Europaean ones that they are hardly distinguishable from them.

As it was the humour of the ship to keep Christmas in the old fashiond way it was resolvd of them to make a Goose pye for tomorrows dinner.

25. Christmas day: Our Goose pye was eat with great approbation and in the Evening all hands were as Drunk as our forefathers usd to be upon the like occasion.

26. This morn all heads achd with yesterdays debauch. Wind has been Easterly these 3 or 4 days so we have not got at all nearer the Island than we were.

*The **Endeavour** Journal of Joseph Banks*

The Festive Season at Port Jackson

1ST. January, 1789. To-day being new-year's-day, most of the officers were invited to the governor's table. Manly dined heartily on fish and roasted pork; he was seated on a chest near a window, out of which, when he had done eating, he would have thrown his plate, had he not been prevented: during dinner-time a band of music played in an adjoining apartment, and after the cloth was removed, one of the company sang in a very soft and superior style; but the powers of melody were lost on Manly, which disappointed our expectations, as he had before shown pleasure and readiness in imitating our tunes. Stretched out on his chest, and putting his hat under his head, he fell asleep.

To convince his countrymen that he had received no injury from us, the governor took him in a boat down the harbour, that they might see and converse with him: when the boat arrived, and lay at a little distance from the beach, several Indians who had retired at her approach, on seeing Manly, returned: he was greatly affected, and shed tears. At length they began to converse. Our ignorance of the language prevented us from knowing much of what passed; it was, however, easily understood that his friends asked him why he did not jump overboard, and rejoin them. He only sighed, and pointed to the fetter on his leg, by which he was bound.

In going down the harbour he had described the names by which they distinguish its numerous creeks and headlands: he was now often heard to repeat that of *Weè-rong* (Sydney), which was doubtless to inform his countrymen of the place of his captivity; and perhaps invite them to rescue him. By this time his gloom was chased away, and he parted from his friends without testifying reluctance. His vivacity and good humour continued all the evening, and produced so good an effect on his appetite, that he eat for supper two Kanguroo rats, each of the size of a moderate rabbit, and in addition not less than three pounds of fish.

The Journals of Captain Watkin Tench

Santa Claus

"Halt! Who goes there?" The sentry's call
Rose on the midnight air
Above the noises of the camp,
The roll of wheels, the horses' tramp.
The challenge echoed over all –
"Halt! Who goes there?"

A quaint old figure clothed in white,
He bore a staff of pine,
An ivy-wreath was on his head.
"Advance, O friend," the sentry said,
"Advance, for this is Christmas Night,
And give the countersign."

"No sign nor countersign have I.
Through many lands I roam
The whole world over far and wide.
To exiles all at Christmastide
From those who love them tenderly
I bring a thought of home.

"From English brook and Scottish burn,
From cold Canadian snows,
From those far lands ye hold most dear
I bring you all a greeting here,
A frond of a New Zealand fern,
A bloom of English rose.

"From faithful wife and loving lass
I bring a wish divine,
For Christmas blessings on your head."
"I wish you well," the sentry said,
"But here, alas! you may not pass
Without the countersign."

He vanished – and the sentry's tramp
Re-echoed down the line.
It was not till the morning light
The soldiers knew that in the night
Old Santa Claus had come to camp
Without the countersign.

A.B. Paterson

14

the
ORATORIO

The first and second parts, together with a portion of the third part, of Handel's Messiah, were given at the Victoria Theatre on Tuesday, for the benefit of the Commercial Reading Rooms and Library. The music had been got up under the direction of Messrs. Johnson, and the performers comprised nearly the whole of the available musical skill of the city.

On the arrival of His Excellency the Governor, who was well received, the National Anthem was sung by the choir, accompanied by the whole orchestra, and the same was repeated at the conclusion.

The Overture was played with considerable taste and precision, which prepared us for our usual treat in the succeeding tenor solo, *"Comfort ye my People"* – when, eheu! out squeaked a shrill *treble*, pitched a *full* octave above the composer's score, and we fancied we heard the ghost of old Handel exclaim, in his well known phrase, "Te teyvil, te teyvil! dat is no ma moosic." What in the name of common sense could tempt Mr. Johnson to suffer the beautiful harmony of this sublime air to be turned upside down in this manner? especially as he had one or two good tenors competent to sing the part.

While thus condemning an inexcusable error, we hasten to express our admiration of the manner in which Mrs. Bushelle sang *"I know that my Redeemer liveth,"* which is one of the finest airs within the whole range of musical composition. Passing over the choruses *"And the Glory of the Lord,"* and *"He shall purify,"* as well as Mr. F. Howson's *"But who may abide,"* in which there was little remarkable, we come to the solo, *"Behold a Virgin shall conceive,"* which was given by Mrs. Gibbs with great accuracy, always excepting her defective articulation of the words. The chorus, *"O thou that tellest,"* went passably well, but Mr. Waller's *"For behold darkness,"* was a little darker, we apprehend, than the composer could have intended or wished. It is but fair to say that this gentleman was very useful in the choruses, for which alone his voice is fitted. The master stroke of the evening was, decidedly, the choral fugue, *"For unto us a child is born."* This, had the number and power of voices been quadrupled, would have been perfect. And truly there is nothing finer extant of its kind.

The *Pastoral Symphony* was beautifully played, and Mrs. Stirling did tolerable justice to the four succeeding recitatives. The chorusses *"Glory to God,"* and *"His yoke is easy,"* were also free from serious objection, and the same might be said of the air *"Rejoice greatly,"* had not Mrs. Busshelle outstripped the modesty of oratorio canons by acting the part.

The exquisite pastoral air *"He shall feed his flock,"* was sung by Madame Carandini with good effect. The other pieces worthy of special remark were *"He was despised,"* beautifully intoned by Mr. J. Howson; *"But thou did'st not leave,"* by Mrs. Wallace, (which as it was sung badly the first time, the audience kindly encored;) *"How beautiful are the feet,"* sung with feeling by Mrs. Stirling; and the Hallelujah Chorus, which last was, we believe, sung *in tune* on this occasion, for the first time in New South Wales. At the last Oratorio, it was actually transformed into an *adagio*.

It may be remarked of the choruses, in general, that the uppermost and lowermost parts were sung with much precision, but that the reverse was the case with respect to the intermediate parts, particularly the altos.

Besides His Excellency the Governor and Lady Gipps, we observed present His Excellency the Commander of the Forces and suite, and the Right Worshipful the Mayor and family. The boxes of the Theatre were crowded with persons of fashion, a proof out of many, that however faulty in some respects the musical taste of the colony may be, it is sufficiently prevalent to be worthy of cultivation and improvement.

The Sydney Morning Herald,
25 December, 1845.

CANDLES
and
CAROLS

Wednesday night's Carols by Candlelight, presented by the Armidale Lions Club in Central Park, was an outstanding success.

Among the crowd which braved the unseasonably cold weather on the night were (pictured) Helen Belshaw, 8 months, with friends Kathy, Carolyn and Veronica Hall and Mrs Ildi Hall.

The president of the Armidale Lions Club, Mr Colin Behrend, said he was extremely pleased with the event and believed the whole evening went off very well.

"The crowd was quite large although the cold weather would have kept many families at home," Mr Behrend said.

"Although it was hard to assess how many people came, the turnout seemed to be rather good."

According to Mr Behrend, donations to the Ministers Fraternal Christmas Bowl were given generously by the public who were not only showing the Christmas spirit through singing.

The Mayor of Armidale, Alderman Rosemary Leitch, gave an address and the Armidale Youth Orchestra and Armidale High School Choir contributed to the success of the night.

The Armidale Express,
20 December, 1988.

17

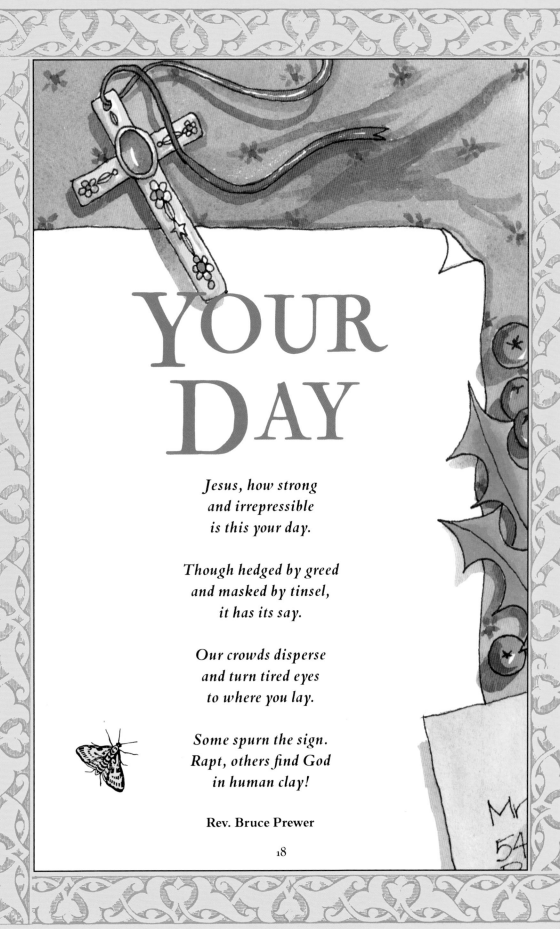

YOUR DAY

Jesus, how strong
and irrepressible
is this your day.

Though hedged by greed
and masked by tinsel,
it has its say.

Our crowds disperse
and turn tired eyes
to where you lay.

Some spurn the sign.
Rapt, others find God
in human clay!

Rev. Bruce Prewer

18

My Dear Edna,

It's been so long since we last met. Wouldn't it be lovely if we could get together for christmas!

Peter and I are coming over to Perth this year. Sandra and her husband will also be in town, so we could meet. Wonderful Blue Sk...

AIR MAIL
PAR
AVION

Edna Brown
Lea... Street
Freema...
...W.A.

CHRISTMAS 1963
PEACE ON EARTH
GOODWILL TO MEN
AUSTRALIA 5d

del Vaga: The Holy Family
Christmas 1978
AUSTRALIA 55c

AUSTRALIA
Behold I bring you good tidings of great joy
5d

...Street
...th.
NSW

Mrs. J. Smith
...rown Street
...url

Colonial Christmas Day

Christmas dinner along the overland stock route across the continent. Sand and a million flies. Sand and flies and the mirage. Thin and blue the smoke of a billy fire drifting straight up in the windless air. Billy fire of an overlander, of a lean, lone overlander, Darwin-bound. Damper for his dinner, his Christmas dinner; but no regret for gayer Christmases seems to shadow his philosophic calm. Calm of philosophy, calm of solitude, calm of the desert, of the brooding grey-green bush. How should one so calm regret a tinsel day, a bon-bon day, like Christmas?

Besides, having lost count of the days, he is under the impression that Christmas is still three days away.

Christmas dawn on the beaches, the curving beaches. Beaches like flower-beds packed with moving flowers. Scarlet, jade, orange, turquoise swimming suits, sunshades, mandarin coats, like parrot-flowers on the dazzle-sanded beaches. Arrowy boys darting erect on surfboards through the foam-smother; jade-suited girls riding curly dolphins, curly sea-dragons made of tinted rubber. Out beyond the breakers, out beyond the laughter, in the surf boat, bronzed, immobile, a life-saver with a spear, a black and savage shark-spear, at his feet.

A Christmas dawn in the mulga, the lonely mulga, in the lonely cottage nineteen miles from nowhere. Early awake is the only child in the cottage, the little girl, so brown, so thin, so grave. Twenty-nine presents has she to distribute to her friends, this brown little girl, nineteen miles from nowhere. Who are her twenty-nine friends so far away, deep in the mulga? Five calves are her friends, two ringtail 'possums, seven small lambs, a paddymelon delicate, quick, a native bear sleepy and slow, two magpies, a sheep dog, eight kittens, a kookaburra, two cockatoos.

Jean Curlewis, 1928.

A Hearty Good Wish

*Bright with gold is
the morning sun
Cool and sweet is
the early dew
Crystal clear is the
song of the lark
Speeding to bring this
message to you*

Dear Virginia...

Last week we reported that the French Post Office had closed down its section handling replies to Santa Claus letters. This week it was revealed that the Australian Post Office is already destroying some 2,000 letters a week sent to Santa by Australian children. At least the Post Office could acknowledge these letters, even if this meant destroying some illusions. It could take a leaf out of the New York "Sun's" book and rephrase their famous editorial of 1897: "Dear Virginia, your little friends are dead right. There *is* no Santa Claus. So stop clogging up the mails, which are slow enough already. (Sgd.) Director-General of Posts and Telegraphs."

If, however, the D.-G. was a stickler for the rules, he could cushion this brutal reply with more official language. "With reference to your letter of 18th inst., directed to 'Claus, S., South Pole, Antarctica, the World, Space,' it is desired to advise that no such person is known at that address. It is regrettably not possible to forward your letter to Greenland and the Faroe Islands, Iceland, Christmas or Cocos (Keeling) Islands or Alaska. This would have required payment of the relevant Customs clearance fee on articles other than parcels, since your communication has been classified as an unsolicited request for the delivery of certain dutiable goods on 25th inst.

"Similar regulations apply to postal articles addressed to Nicholas, Saint (being a deceased person) and Christmas, Father (not being a member of any bona fide religious order under Section 26 of the Act). Since you have not applied for return of your letter, with prepayment of the relevant surcharge for underpaid mail by the parent or guardian of a minor having custody of the minor, we regret to advise that your letter has been destroyed. With seasonal good wishes from the Postmaster-General."

Sydney Morning Herald,
21 December, 1968.

Father Christmas lives at the North Pole with lots of Penguins

Cure for Drunkenness

A man who had been sacrificing a little too freely at the shrine of the jolly god on Christmas Day, and who had not recovered his proper senses on the following morning, was wending his way through the market-place when, unfortunately, he was encountered by some wags, full of fun and frolic, who persuaded him that they had received instructions from the Chief Police Magistrate to exalt him in the market-place for his delinquency. This they immediately put in execution by obliging him to mount that formidable machine y'clept the pillory, in which he remained fixed for some time, exposed to the hootings of the mob, which was numerously collected on the occasion.

Sydney Times,
30 December, 1834.

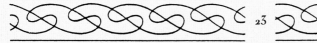

Christmas with my Prodigal True Love

O *n the first day of Christmas/My true love sent to me/A partridge in a pear tree.*

That is the first verse of the Christmas song "The Twelve Days of Christmas" which lists a huge amount of livestock, gifts and people that an infatuated young man once sent to his true love.

The song is traditional and no one really knows when it was written, but any love-lorn young man contemplating sending the articles listed in the song to his true love this Christmas had better be very, very rich.

When it is all added up, the young man sends to his true love the following:
12 partridges in 12 pear trees
22 turtle doves
30 French hens
36 calling birds
40 gold rings
42 geese a-laying
42 swans a-swimming
40 maids a-milking
36 ladies dancing
30 Lords a-leaping
22 pipers piping
12 drummers drumming.

To estimate the cost of this lot is no mean task but this week I attempted it.

Pear trees should be easy to find and they are – if you buy them in June. They transplant easily then and most suburban nurseries have them for $1.35 each.

Partridges don't inhabit Sydney in large numbers, even Taronga Zoo has only two, so I was faced with the problem (theoretical) of importing 12 birds from England.

Miss Barbara Purse, Taronga Zoo's Press Officer, supplied the information that partridges cost $120 a pair to import. The price she said, includes freight.

Turtle doves are $4 each at the Campsie Animal Centre and Aquarium Pty. Ltd. The manager, Mr A. Murphy, said they only had one pair at the moment but they could fill an order for 22 if given some notice.

A French hen, I was told, is simply a breed of domestic hen. Summerleaves Livestock Farm Pty. Ltd. can supply young laying hens for only $2 each. It might seem like cheating but I had to compromise.

Calling birds are Peacocks and

again Barbara Purse from Taronga Zoo came up with a price.

One hundred dollars each – imported from England.

At most city jewellers, gold rings range from $12 up. Prouds said they could supply 40 very attractive, plain gold rings for $50 each.

Geese were a problem. After many unsuccessful enquiries, I could not find anyone in Sydney who breeds geese commercially.

However, down in Tasmania there is a native bird called the Cape Barren Goose.

I decided to poach 42 of these and risk the $10 (per bird) fine for having a protected bird in my possession.

The same applied to swans. The native black swan was the bird I was after, but a spokesman for the National Parks and Wildlife Service said I would face the same $10 fine for each of them.

Maids a-milking requires both maids and cows. Dalgety and New Zealand Loan Ltd. said Friesian cows were selling for $200 each with an option of "calf at foot" if I wanted them.

With the school holidays in full swing, 40 schoolgirl milkmaids could be expected to answer an advertisement offering $10 for a day of milking.

Ladies dancing are also hard to find but if you could hire the dancers from every nightclub in Sydney and Melbourne there would be almost 36.

A spokesman for the Lido in Melbourne said dancers were $12 each a night with first class air travel and accommodation.

So 36 dancers should average $20 each a day.

Lords a-leaping was the biggest stumbling block. The Lords I contacted in Sydney declined to leap for any price but one suggested that some of the younger Lords in England could be hired for $1,000 a day.

Qantas said the return first-class air fare from England to Australia via Europe and Asia was $1,950 (single).

Leaping Lords would insist on first-class accommodation so I allowed $100 a day for each Lord.

The secretary of the Parramatta Caledonian Society Pipe Band, Mr N. Jewell, told me that I would need two bands to get 22 pipers and 12 drummers.

He said they would cost at least $100 a day each.

With all the information gathered and all items priced, it only remained to find the sum total.

For convenience, I assumed that our infatuated young man would economise and send everything for the last day only.

This reduces the cost as accommodation charges become overnight only rather than for four days.

The total cost, presuming that the young lady has a swimming pool for the swans to swim in, is $108,144.20.

I am glad my inquiries were only theoretical, otherwise I would not be smiling until about Christmas 2010 when all the loans had been paid off.

David D. McNicoll
***Sun-Herald**, 21 December, 1969.*

MEMORIES *of* CHRISTMAS

*I*t was at Christmas time that my aunts' gifts came fully into their own and with the largish families of those days there were plenty of young fry on which their unselfish labours could be exercised. After Church the grandchildren and their parents arrived and of course were indulged in the huge, hot dinner which we continued to cook so unsuitable to our climate. We children, anxious to secure *some* trophy from the pudding, even though it were only the batchelor's button or the spinster's thimble, prolonged our efforts until the desired end had been attained. Then, as if almonds and raisins, etc. did not make us sufficiently replete, we went out on the lawn where watermelon au naturel was served to cool us down; cooled to the ears we had a short rest before tackling further joys. The interest of the dinner was greatly heightened by the place-cards, designed of course by our talented aunts, with a humorous caricature of the person concerned and a witty verse with reference to some outstanding characteristic or some event during the year. The uncles would take us on during the afternoon and do their best to dissipate the effects of over-indulgence by the all round games like twos and threes, drop the handkerchief and oranges and lemons which gave a satisfactory amount of exercise to young and old. After an evening meal, cold this time, the Christmas presents were given out, ours being supposed to be made by ourselves. Our aunts' originality was again displayed in the way the presents were distributed, sometimes out of a snowball, sometimes from a post office, sometimes just Father Christmas himself. After this a lot of parlour games, spin the platter, hunt the slipper, charades, etc. and finally Christmas hymns with good effect for most, from my grandfather down had tuneful voices. Then off we went home after what might be considered a thoroughly well-spent day. On Boxing Day our family returned the compliment by entertaining the grandmother, aunts and uncles and this was one of the occasions when we had reason to be grateful for the proximity of Tristrams ginger-beer factory, perhaps for ourselves rather than the grandmother.

Eleanor E. Bourne, 1893.

Carol of the
Birds

Out on the plains the Brolgas are dancing,
Lifting their feet like war-horses prancing:
Up to the sun the woodlarks go winging,
Faint in the dawn light echoes their singing
Orana! Orana! Orana to Christmas Day.

Down where the tree-ferns grow by the river,
There where the waters sparkle and quiver,
Deep in the gullies Bell-birds are chiming,
Softly and sweetly their lyric notes rhyming –
Orana! Orana! Orana to Christmas Day.

Friar birds sip the nectar of flowers,
Currawongs chant in wattle-tree bowers;
In the blue ranges Lorikeets calling –
Carols of bushbirds rising and falling –
Orana! Orana! Orana to Christmas Day.

John Wheeler

CHRISTMAS FARE

Colonial Goose

Leg or a shoulder of mutton, boned
3 ozs finely chopped bacon
1 teaspoon finely chopped parsley
3 ozs fresh breadcrumbs
8 tablespoons finely chopped onion
1 teaspoon mixed herbs, thyme, sage
*   and marjoram*
½ teaspoon freshly grated nutmeg
½ teaspoon grated lemon rind
salt and pepper to taste
1 well-beaten egg
milk

Mix all the ingredients together except the egg and milk. Add the egg and enough milk just to moisten the ingredients. Stuff the opening in the meat and tie securely.

Heat a little fat or butter in a roasting pan and brown the meat all over. Roast in a medium to hot oven, allowing fifteen to twenty minutes to the pound depending on how well done you like it.

To serve, cut off strings and lay meat on a heated platter; surround with baby boiled potatoes or small roast potatoes. Serve with gravy handed separately in a sauce boat. Serves eight.

Mrs Roberts' Christmas Cake 1900

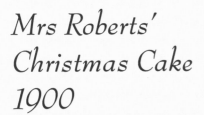

1 lb sugar
1 lb butter
8 eggs
1 lb sultanas
1 lb currants
1 lb raisins
18 ozs flour
½ lb blanched almonds
½ lb peel
1 flat teaspoon of bicarbonate of soda
1 small teaspoon nutmeg
1 full teaspoon cinnamon
½ teaspoon ratafia
1 teaspoon mixed spice
2 teaspoons of lemon essence

Beat sugar and butter to a cream. Add eggs one at a time and beat between eggs. Then add a little fruit and a little flour alternately. Have your fruit in one tin and your flour (with spices added) in another tin. Put in the bicarb. soda with the butter and the sugar. Tie about twenty thicknesses of paper outside the tin. Put cake in a very slow oven for about four to four and a half hours.

OPERATION CHRISTMAS PUDDING

*C*ar and trail bike accidents, childbirth, broken bones and the occasional gunshot or knife wound are all in a day's work for the flying doctors of far western New South Wales.

But there's one day each year when the doctors have other, weightier problems to attend to.

It's the day the doctors take to the air with a precious cargo for two remote outback hospitals at Wilcannia and Ivanhoe.

The safe delivery of crates of Christmas puddings is top priority and the flying medics haven't missed a delivery date yet.

Broken Hill's now famous puddings have been despatched to far-flung corners of the globe and, closer to home, Sydney, Melbourne and Canberra. In Adelaide, ex-patriate Broken-Hillites have a regular standing order for their puddings.

The tradition began back in 1956 when the women's auxiliary for the Royal Flying Doctor Service decided to make a few puddings to raise money for the medical service. In the '50s and '60s, the women produced the puddings in their own kitchens.

These days, the seven-day cook-in could be likened to army manoeuvres. When pudding convenor Val Anderson joined the women's auxiliary in 1975, a giant kitchen was set up in the deserted Broken Hill Hospital pathology department. Two moves later, the Zinc Corporation offered the group a vacant cafeteria and that's where they hope to stay.

Because the post of pudding convenor is such an important one, Val moves into the city for the fortnight from her bush property.

"I'm the first in and the last to leave for two weeks," she says.

It's one delivery
the flying doctors wouldn't like
to miss out on...

This year, the 35 members of the auxiliary produced 1860 Christmas puddings. Most were already spoken for, but those that weren't went like the proverbial hot cakes on the two selling days. The mailman delivered others to outback stations and local stock and station agencies helped out with deliveries.

Every woman in the group has a routine on cooking days. Some mix the 230 kg of raisins, sultanas and currants, others take care of the 336 dozen eggs, butter and flour and the lucky ones get to mix the 29 flagons of brandy into the 16 big coppers.

"It's the best job of all. They put on their rubber gloves and dive into it. Their reward is to sit down at the end of the day and clean themselves up," Val laughed.

The women come from far and wide to help out. One drives 360 km each day, others come in from their properties and a couple move into the city for the two weeks.

Last year's pudding profit came to more than $6,000. This year, all going to plan, the auxiliary hopes to raise around $8,000 for the Flying Doctor Service.

And what makes the puddings so special? "I guess," says Val, "they're just like the ones grandma used to make."

*Lyn White, **Women's Weekly,** December, 1987.*

DECORATIONS GALORE

In the Christmas selling period of 1987, David Jones sold the following quantities of seasonal items:

3,700 Christmas trees, 301,000 (10,300 sets) Christmas tree lights, 10,000 glass baubles, 73,000 metres tinsel, 320,000 metres wrapping paper, 608,000 metres ribbon, and 1.4 million Christmas cards.

Days of Excess

If you've an eye for Christmas-orientated statistics, Australia is a mighty fine place to study. You'd discover, for example, that 1.75 million Australians had turkey on Tuesday, and that 4,700 tonnes of ham were consumed that day across the nation.

Your calculator's silicon chip would be suffering after working out the cost of the 30 million bon-bons which festive Anzacs cracked on the 25th, or how much money changed hands buying the odd 300,000 bottles of imported liqueurs Australians acquired during December.

Your slide-rule would have a hangover working out the commercial profit gathered from the three million kilograms of dried fruits that were eaten on Tuesday, the $1.5 million spent on one manufacturer's plum puddings alone, or the 250,000 artificial trees which were decorated on suburban hearths.

Although figures have not been collected on the extent of retail sales this year, the Retail Traders' Association believed that sales over Christmas were "good", although it "was not a boom year".

Last minute Christmas shoppers spent an estimated $80 million on Monday.

The deputy managing director of Australia's only $2,000 million retailer, the Coles/K Mart group, Mr Bevan Bradbury, said last Saturday that the group's chain stores and supermarkets had reported excellent sales over the previous 10 days.

"But our experience suggests that even Friday's figures will be eclipsed in Monday's rush," he said.

Coles prepared for the onslaught with a massive restocking operation after Saturday's trading.

If you sat down on Tuesday night after collecting statistics, and after swallowing one of the five million bubbly Alka-Seltzer tablets tumbling down overfed Australians' throats, you could be forgiven for not caring how far the 20,000 km of gift-wrapping paper used in Australia would stretch (from Melbourne to London) or how much the post office made from the 130 million Christmas cards posted in the last frantic days ($19.5 million).

But you could not ignore the most saddening, sickening statistic of all – the road toll – which showed too many Australians ignored the advice given by The Age newspaper three days before Christmas Day: "Certainly, eat drink and be merry – but take a taxi home."

Australian Express (London), 28 December, 1979.

Barking up the Wrong Tree

When we put up the Christmas tree last year, Pip, our year-young golden labrador, squatted beside it and trotted off without telling us. Through sheer olfactory detection we discovered her festive gesture some hours later, but it was patently clear she could see nothing wrong in her action. It was this performance that, for a little while earned her the nickname the Old Factory.

We got the same plastic tree down from the attic last week and prayed there would not be a repeat performance. There wasn't. Instead, she tried to eat the baubles before becoming momentarily hypnotised by the flashing lights. She was snapped out of the trance by a single trigger word: biscuit.

She is a year older now and considers actions like squatting beneath Christmas trees crass and juvenile, a deed reserved for puppies. Baubles and fairy lights are more fun.

My wife came home with two bright woollen Christmas stockings which we suspended from the archway that separates the living room from the dining room. For a full 15 minutes Pip sat directly beneath the garments and barked at them as they dangled just a few centimetres above her nose.

It's fatal to place anything vaguely tempting under the tree or anywhere for that matter. Last December when we threw our annual Christmas barbecue she quietly lifted 11 sausages from a plate. She swallowed them whole – we know this for certain because she regurgitated them intact, still strung together.

She stole something again last night, but the singularly annoying thing is that we haven't a clue what it was. She would have got clean away with it were it not for a Made in Taiwan sticker on her nose.

Christmas 1984, she was only a few weeks old and I was in the throes of teaching her to 'go' in the garden rather than in the house and beneath the Christmas tree. Getting nowhere fast I turned to Brian the vet, my old friend with whom I went through school.

"Judge when she wants to do her thing, take her outside and give a trigger word that she will associate with…well, doing her thing," he suggested, before charging me the usual coldie at my place.

That night Pip began whimpering at 2 am. Leaping out of bed I ushered her out into the back garden. As she sniffed around in the darkness, I urged her on. "Come on girl. Whizzie, whizzie. Whizzie, whizzie. Whizzie, whizzie."

That's how I got to meet the new neighbour. He has since told me that he had been observing me for at least 10 minutes pacing the back yard saying, "Whizzie, whizzie. Whizzie, whizzie", but because of the darkness was unable to see the dog. He still looks at me strangely.

Right now Pip looks quite cute and innocent, snoring away under the table. She'll be three next Christmas. That's 21 in human years. I suppose she'll want a party. I'll get some sausages in.

*John Allin, **The Age**, 23 December, 1986.*

The Queenslander Illustrated Xmas Supplement for 1897

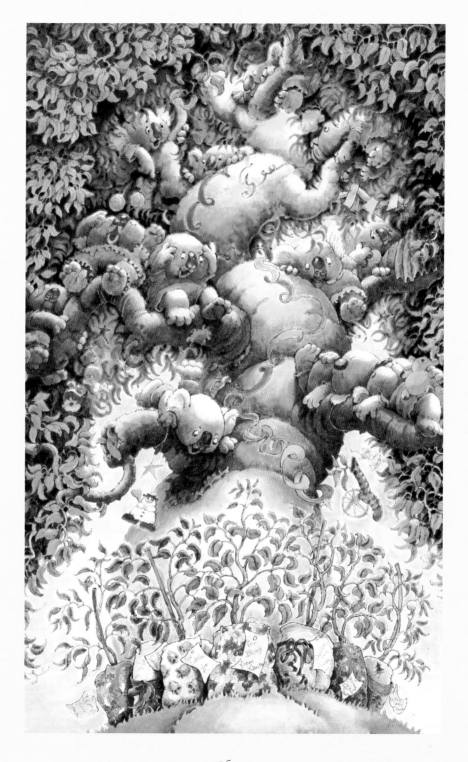

EUCALYPTUS CHRISTMAS

The native born koala lives

inside a eucalyptus.

He sleeps in it at night and then

he eats his bed for breakfast.

His morning tea is eucalypt,

then eucalyptus brunch.

Perhaps he'll pick some eucalypt

just in time for lunch.

Dinner will be similar,

supper's eucalyptus,

And then he can look forward to

A Eucalyptus Christmas!

Stephen Axelsen

By Fast Train

One major problem in writing an account of the Hobart Race is that after a day or two of post-race partying in Constitution Dock and environs it's hard to remember your own name, let alone what happened on the boat.

Now, what was the name of the boat? (Quick look at the T-shirt.) Ah, *Starlight Express*; there are a few brain cells left. To Hobart on the Davidson 55 *Starlight Express*.

This was the right year to go on a big boat. Of course we don't know that at the CYC dock on Boxing Day. But it is already clear that this will be a well-run show, with some excellent sailors amongst the crew of 16, including sail-maker, rigger and the entire crew of one of the Sydney 18 ft skiffs, new sails, lots of food and some good-looking bunks (none of this one tonner sleep-on-the-rail caper, thanks).

First mission of the day is – will the skipper Ian Treleaven let me bring a pillow on board? Yes! I will live in comfort!

Next mission – is there still time to squeeze back down the dock to the clubhouse? The crush is unbelievable; one of these years the whole lot will surely subside into the waves. Relatives visiting the CYC for the first time to see us off probably think it's like this every Saturday in the glamorous world of yachting.

It's a relief to motor away from the marina and out to the Heads to see what is in store – a light but building nor'easter.

We've got time to kill so I duck down below to unwrap my new Musto wet weather gear, regulation on this boat because Ian runs Musto NZ and Australia. He would have loaned me some but what the hell, it's Christmas.

I've bought some of the Musto thermal underwear, too, and that's going to prove to be one of the few smart things I've done all year as the race progresses.

The final countdown begins. We will be starting on the forward line for the big boats and Southern Cross Cup fleet and as we begin to make our approach we seem to come in rather too fast. It looks like we're going to be early. We're too bloody early!

Everyone starts to scream and shout (funny when you notice your own voice amongst the chorus). Ian stalls the boat, then just squeezes down across the bows of two leeward yachts and the cannon fires. Now we'll have to wait 20 minutes before they broadcast recalls over the radio.

It's all action with the maxis powering away to weather and the little boats ducking and weaving like a swarm of bees behind us out of the second start line blocks.

I've got a hand-held radio set in my hand and headphones on because we're supposed to talk to Channel 10 at some stage. I suspect this is not going to work out for the best, though it's entertaining in a bizarre way to be simultaneously sailing in the race and listening to a commentary about it.

My suspicions are confirmed when we tack and I have to abandon the radio onto the aft cockpit floor to man the genoa winch. A wave comes aboard heading straight for the radio, which drowns.

No, hang on, it starts to work again just as we reach the limits of the eastern shore spectator fleet. Rambo wants to charge on in and scatter them, but Ian tacks and the radio gets dumped again. This time a wave really has its number and the poor thing curls up its antenna and dies. Channel 10 this is *Starlight Express*, over and *out*.

During the afternoon I'm supposed to talk to the Sydney radio station 2GB, but now that we're into the Strait we can't get a clear enough line to do so in spite

This was the right year to go on a big boat.

of Sydney Radio's efforts. The crew are disappointed because it means I've been unable to find out the score in the Aust v NZ cricket Test. *Starlight* is built and registered in NZ, but on this trip the Kiwis on board are outnumbered 13 to three.

Though the other watch are more subdued now they find a new way to keep us awake by turning wave jumping into an art form. *Starlight* doesn't mind; she feels strong enough to take anything. But for us poor suckers inside her there's the feeling of having left your stomach behind as the boat lifts over a wave, a moment of freefall and then bash! And again, bash! bash! bash! until it's a relief to come back on deck.

We're still eating well thanks to Susie's pre-preparation of easily handled stuff like trays of jaffles. It's cold, but I'm feeling most snug and self-satisfied in my new thermal gear.

Now comes a night of sail changes as the southerly lightens, kicks back in from time to time to give the foredeck guys something to do and then dies completely when we're caught inside the rhumb line off Bicheno. At midnight we're becalmed, then find a little bit of pressure by sailing due east for an hour. It doesn't feel right, but maybe there's more wind out to sea and there's also some form of perverse pleasure in not having to look at the S on the compass card just for a change.

Eventually we do find more breeze and can come back down to course under spinnaker and then light genoa as the wind clocks from north to sou'west. By daylight we're close reaching past Maria Island in a gentle breeze. Sailing with a crew of 16 has its up and down sides. With seven or eight people on each watch there often aren't enough jobs to go around, but on the other hand there's always plenty of manpower and even enthusiasm for sail changes, so the boat is driven hard all the way. Meanwhile it's time for scones, jam and cream – and that's no lie!

Here comes the aerial photographer Richard Bennett and his pilot, who seem to share a death wish. Their aircraft sideslips on its kamikaze course for our backstay, somehow misses, then turns so slowly for another pass that we wait for it to fall out of the sky.

As we enter the Derwent the tide is against us and the breeze really starts to fade so we keep gybing back into the eastern shore with our local expert Susie on the helm. The finish line finally comes into view; we *are* going to make it before the southerly dies. People start taking turns to go below to change into their *Starlight* shirts and everyone now thinks it's a damn shame that the boats behind us will run out of breeze.

We cross the line at 19h 51m 54s, having made it from Tasman Island in not much more than four hours and averaging about 8 kts for the whole race. The next boat won't arrive until after midnight. There are five masts already at the dock. *Helsal II* has beaten us after all, along with the maxis *Sovereign*, *Apollo* and *Gazebo* and that bloody *Rager* which has made it to spite the cynics.

The dock is crowded with people we don't know and they all start clapping as we come in beside *Rager*. It's a little bit unnerving and hard to know where to look, particularly when we bump into the dock and smash our nav lights.

We're a day early – no one's booked accommodation for the 29th. Next day there'll be the knowledge that we've been lucky with the weather but also the feeling that the boat has been well run and driven hard and also a sense of pride in seeing her mast dwarfed by much larger ones to either side.

Meanwhile, next day is far away. Look out world, it's time for the Customs House and Maloney's.

Vanessa Dudley,
Australian Sailing,
February, 1988.

Christmas
IN TWO LANDS

There *it is cold, or there is snow –*
And holly, fires and mistletoe,
And carols sung out in the street
By children, walking through the sleet.
Church bells break the frozen air
Ringing loudly everywhere.
There *is where white winter glory*
Comes to tell the Christmas story.

Here it is hot, the sun is gold –
And turns tired when day is old,
Christmas carols are sung at night
Somewhere outside, by candle-light.
Church bells ring out in the heat
And call to people in the street.
The Christmas story here is told
In summer, when the sun is gold.

Joan Mellings

They Celebrated With Feasting

Everyone carried something. Mark took the tucker box, and Lonny and the girls took the rug, tablecloth and cushions. Father took charge of the tea billy and the key task of lighting the fire. There was a stone fireplace, most civilised. Ella and Aunty Clair and Boo showed Bea and Jenny where was the best place on the grass to spread the tablecloth. They moved it several times. The first place was too shady, the second was too much in the sun, and at the third place there were ants. Mother dissociated herself from the decision-making. She walked from shrub to flower, naming things, gloating over them. She discovered a deodar tree from the Himalayas, and a South African protea and a cedar of Lebanon. She found a tree with foliage like softest moss, which she said was from New Zealand, and rare in the extreme.

"What do you think of this position, Letty?" called Aunty Clair to her. "Oh very good, very good," said Mother without looking.

So they refrained from bothering Mother with a thing so trivial as choosing a picnic spot for Christmas dinner, and chose it themselves. They at last settled on a patch of velvet grass, half-sun and half-shade, reasonably level and with the minimum population of ants. Here they spread the big cloth of white damask. It had a patch or two, for it had belonged to

Grandmother Wilkins, but it was starched and crisp. They spread it with never a wrinkle.

On the rather bumpy white expanse, they arrayed their feast: the leg of lamb, the potato salad, the home-baked bread and child-churned butter; and the cold Christmas pudding.

"It's ready," called Aunty Clair. "Teddy, go and fetch your father. Boo, does your mother know the food is waiting? We are ready to eat."

Mother, under the deodar tree,

of his, then close it again.

"May the Lord make us truly thankful," prayed Mother.

In many a place, round about now, there would be people with at least one eye closed, perhaps two, feeling thankful, and blessed.

The food tasted wonderful. It was festive food: once-a-year food. The pudding had to be eaten in solemn silence. Otherwise, there was a danger of swallowing one of those silver pieces that Mother had been saving. Trust Boo to find the sixpence in her slice of pudding.

had to drag herself back from the Himalayas. Father was found, fascinated by a water pump, which worked itself endlessly by the small lake. Flowing water kept it moving, beating out the pulse of the living stream.

"It'll keep going forever, that pump," said Father. Teddy led him back to the repast.

"I'll say grace," said Mother.

They closed their eyes. Teddy shut hers tight. But she opened one of them, and saw Father open one

Mark had found a trouser button. But no doubt there are times when a trouser button is more useful than a sixpence.

So, only needing to remove the occasional ant or gumnut or piece of twig from the food, they celebrated their Christmas with feasting.

Hesba Brinsmead-Hungerford, 1983.

Christmas is a Thousand Things

It's a winter's night by the Northern sky, a summer's night down South. It's an angel song…a giant star and a tiny stable…a manger, and straw, and swaddling clothes.

Christmas is a chime…a boy soprano and Silent Night…carolers and the First Noel… the tinkle of a bell from Santa's sleigh, of a coin in a cup.

Christmas is Dickens and Scrooge and Tiny Tim. It's holly on the door, a candle in the window, and the sparkle of tinsel.

Christmas is red and green, and blue and silver. Christmas too is white.

Christmas is cards and ribbon and tissue paper. It's a trip home, an open latch and a handclasp. It's giblets and biscuits…turkey and mincemeat pie.

Christmas is forgiveness and a smile.

Christmas is a prayer…a renewed plea for an ancient hope.

For Peace on Earth, Goodwill Toward Men.

The West Australian,
25 December, 1957.

Christmas Bells

Christ-mas Bells ring - ing, Christ-mas Bells ring - ing,

Swing-ing and ring - ing, Oh what do they say?

"Christ-mas is giv - ing time, Christ-mas is lov-ing time,

Giv - ing time, lov - ing time," That's what they say.

Zoe McHenry
(setting by Margaret Moore)

Acknowledgements

TEXT

Australian Consolidated Press Ltd for "Operation Christmas Pudding", *Women's Weekly*, December, 1987.

Chappell & Intersong Music Group (Aust) Ltd for "Carol of the Birds" by John Wheeler and William James.

Joan Mellings for "Christmas in Two Lands" which appeared in *The Sugar-Plum Christmas Book*, compiled by Jean Chapman, Hodder & Stoughton (Aust.) Pty Ltd, 1977.

John Oxley Library, State Library of Queensland for "Memories of Christmas" from the Bourne Family papers.

The Lutheran Publishing House for "Your Day" by Rev. Bruce Prewer, author of *Australian Psalms*, 1979.

McPhee Gribble for recipes of "Colonial Goose" and "Mrs. Roberts Christmas Cake" which appeared in *The Australian Christmas in Days Gone By*, 1982.

Penguin Books Australia Ltd for "Christmas in Sydney 1844" from *Notes & Sketches of N.S.W.* by Mrs. Chas. Meredith, (John Murray, London, 1844, facsimile edition, Penguin, Vic. 1973.)

Angus & Robertson Publishers for: "Santa Claus" by A. B. Paterson which appeared in *The Collected Verse of A. B. Paterson*, 44th edition 1980; "They Celebrated With Feasting" from *Christmas at Longtime* by Hesba Brinsmead-Hungerford, 1983; extracts from "The Journal of Captain Watkin Tench" as reproduced in *Sydney's First Four Years*, (ed. L. F. Hardinge), published in association with The Royal Australian Historical Society (Sydney, 1961.)

Vanessa Dudley for "By Fast Train" which appeared in *Australian Sailing*, February, 1988.

Mitchell Library, State Library of NSW and the Library Council of NSW for entries from "The Endeavour Journal of Joseph Banks" edited by J. C. Beaglehole.

John Fairfax & Sons Ltd for: "The Oratorio" which appeared in the *Sydney Morning Herald* of 25 December, 1845; "Colonial Christmas Day" from *Christmas in Australia* by Jean Curlewis, (Art in Australia Ltd, 1928); "Dear Virginia" from *Sydney Morning Herald* of 21 December, 1968.

David Martin for "Bush Christmas" which appeared in *The Penguin Book of Australian Ballads*, ed. Russel Ward, 1967.

David D. McNicoll for "Christmas with my prodigal true love" printed in the *Sun-Herald*, 21 December, 1969.

The Age for "Barking up the wrong tree at Christmas" by John Allin, 23 December, 1986.

David Jones (Aust.) Pty Ltd for information on 1987 Christmas merchandise sales.

TNT Magazine, London, for "Days of Excess" printed on 28 December, 1979.

The West Australian for "Christmas is a Thousand Things" and "Women of the Outback" which both appeared on 25 December, 1957.

Armidale Express for "Candles and Carols Warm Our Hearts" which appeared on 20 December, 1988.

ASSISTANCE

Staff of the Dixson Library, Armidale campus, and staff of the Historical Resources Unit, Newling campus, of University of New England, Armidale.

Staff of the Armidale and District Memorial Library.

Staff of the John Oxley Library, State Library of Queensland, especially Helen Cole and Diane Burn.

Roy Pugh of the Queensland Card Collectors Society.

Peter Axton and Kathy McAuliffe of Valentine Sands Pty Ltd.

Bob Ross, editor of *Australian Sailing*.

Noel Hosking of Fred Hosking Pty. Ltd.

Shirley Watkins of Hodder & Stoughton (Aust.) Pty Ltd.

Mimi Colligan of Post Office Headquarters and Pauline Hyde of West Armidale Post Office.

Peg McColl of Penguin Books Australia Ltd.

Pamela Laycock of New England Regional Art Museum, Armidale.

P. R. Allen of John Fairfax & Sons Ltd.

Oscar Christiansen of City of Brisbane Lions Club Inc.

Shirley Humphries, Deputy Mitchell Librarian, State Library of NSW.

D. Peachey of David Jones (Aust.) Pty Ltd.

Vanessa Dudley.

Rosalie, Tom & Chris Spalding.

Lloyd Frazier.

Bob Hardie & Chris Barnden for photography.

Special thanks to Sam Elder.

ILLUSTRATIONS

Australia Post for all postage stamps.

Roland Harvey Studios for card (p. 2).

Queensland Card Collectors Society for cards (p. 15 & 21).

Permanent Trustee Company, trustees of the estate of the late Margaret Preston for her painting, "Christmas Bush", and also the Trustees of the New England Regional Art Museum, Armidale (p. 7).

Pro Hart for his painting, "Catching the Xmas Roast" (p. 11).

John Oxley Library, State Library of Queensland, for b/w prints of "Christmas in the Far West" (p. 20). "The Christmas Pudding" (p. 31). "A Strain from the Bush" (p. 35).

Ray Chapman for first Australian Christmas card (cover).

City of Brisbane Lions Club Inc. for Lions Seals of 1984 & 1986 (p. 47).

Accord Publications plc for card (p. 22).

David Jones (Aust.) Pty Ltd for 1989 Christmas display (p. 32).

Vanessa Dudley for Sydney-Hobart Yacht Race transparency (p. 40).

Armidale Express for photograph (p. 17).

Deborah Niland for illustrations (p. 41) from The Sugar Plum Christmas Book compiled by Jean Chapman, Hodder & Stoughton (Aust) Pty Ltd, 1977.

Stephen Axelsen for illustration and poem (pp. 36-7) from *Eucalyptus Christmas*, Hodder & Stoughton (Aust) Pty Ltd, 1983.

John Tourrier for illustrations (p. 38, 39).

Dover Publications, New York, for: decorative borders and ornament (pp. 3, 5, 6-7, 12-21, 23, 27-9, 32-3, 42-3) from *Florid Victorian Ornament* by Karl Klimsch; illustrations (endpapers, pp. 16, 24, 30, 31, 34, 44, 45) from *Catchpenny Prints, 163 Popular Engravings from the Eighteenth Century* (originally published by Bowles & Carver); illustrations (pp. 1, 2, 6, 12, 17, 18, 23, 25) from *1800 Woodcuts by Thomas Bewick and his School*, edited by Blanche Cirker and the editorial staff of Dover Publications.

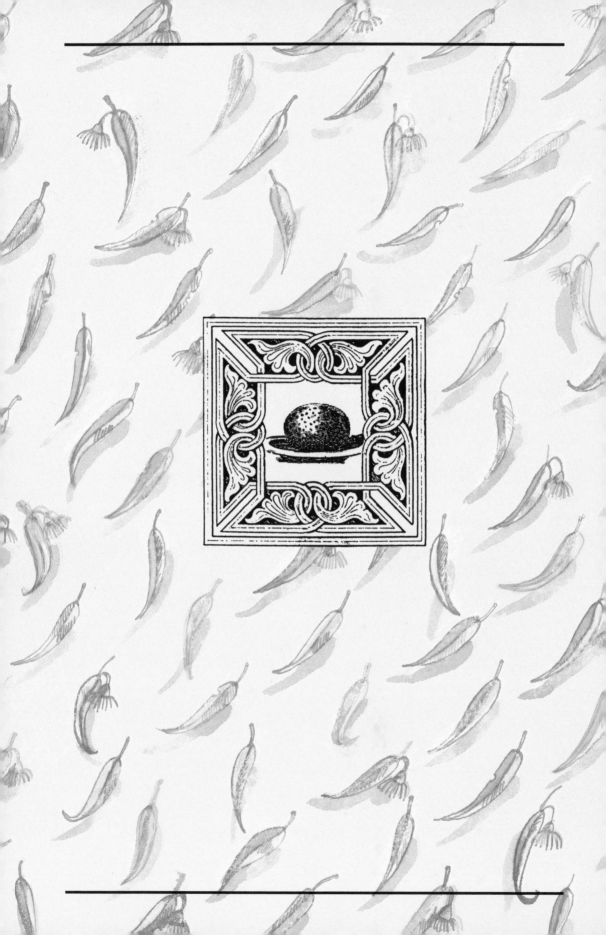